Celebration Days

Celebrating Christian FESTIVALS

NICK HUNTER

raintree

a Capstone company — publishers for children

Raintree is an imprint of Capstone Global Library Limited, a company incorporated in England and Wales having its registered office at 7 Pilgrim Street, London, EC4V 6LB – Registered company number: 6695582

www.raintree.co.uk
myorders@raintree.co.uk

Edited by James Benefield
Designed by Steve Mead
Original illustrations © Capstone Global Library Limited
Illustrated by HL Studios
Picture research by Eric Gohl
Production by Helen McCreath
Originated by Capstone Global Library Limited
Printed and bound in China

ISBN 978 1 406 29770 6
19 18 17 16 15
10 9 8 7 6 5 4 3 2 1

British Library Cataloguing in Publication Data
A full catalogue record for this book is available from the British Library.

Acknowledgements
Alamy: Blend Images, 18, Graham Harrison, 29, Kumar Sriskandan, 12, Marmaduke St. John, 33; Capstone Studio: Karon Dubke, 14–15 (all), 26–27 (all), 36–37 (all); Corbis: Bettmann, 19; Getty Images: Franco Origlia, 31, Heritage Images, 38, Thomas Chatelard, 13, Uriel Sinai, 11; Glow Images: Superstock, 28, Westend61, 9; Newscom: EPA/Dennis M. Sabangan, 17, Picture Alliance/Godong/Philippe Lissac, 39, Toby Adamson, 42, UIG Universal Images Group/Godong, 8, ZUMA Press/National News, 21; Shutterstock: AAR Studio, 43 (right), Air Images, 25, Alexey Anashkin, 41, alexsol, 34, Algefoto, 20, Andre Durao, 16, emei, 24, jorisvo, 4, Kichigin, 40, Kobby Dagan, cover, Nightman1965, 23, Pack-Shot, 10, Patrick Poendl, 32, stocksolutions, 43 (left), tama2012, 22, Vladimir Volodin, 44; SuperStock: National Geographic/Tino Soriano, 35

Design Elements: Shutterstock

We would like to thank Peggy Morgan for her invaluable help in the preparation of this book.

Every effort has been made to contact copyright holders of material reproduced in this book. Any omissions will be rectified in subsequent printings if notice is given to the publisher.

All the internet addresses (URLs) given in this book were valid at the time of going to press. However, due to the dynamic nature of the internet, some addresses may have changed, or sites may have changed or ceased to exist since publication. While the author and publisher regret any inconvenience this may cause readers, no responsibility for any such changes can be accepted by either the author or the publisher.

SAFETY TIPS FOR THE RECIPES
Trying new recipes is fun, but before you start working in the kitchen, keep these safety tips in mind:
- Always ask an adult for permission, especially when using the hob, oven or sharp knives.
- At the hob, always point saucepan handles away from the edge. Don't keep flammable materials, such as towels, too close to the burners. Have a fire extinguisher nearby. Don't lean too close when you lift a lid off a pan – steam can cause burns, too. Always use oven gloves when taking dishes out of the oven.
- Wash your hands before you work, and wash your workspace and utensils after you are done. Cook foods completely. Don't use expired or spoiled food. Be careful when you cut with knives.
- Work with an adult – together you can both learn about religions of the world through food!

CONTENTS

Some words are shown in bold, **like this**. You can find out what they mean by looking in the glossary.

Introducing Christianity

Christianity is a religion based on the teachings of Jesus Christ. Most Christians believe that there is one God experienced in three different ways: as creator of the world, in the human form of Jesus Christ and as a **spiritual** power in the world at all times. Faith in God and loving God and other people are very important to Christians.

The Christian holy book is the Bible, which is divided into two main sections: the Old and New Testaments. Christians share much of the Bible with Judaism, but hey do not share the New Testament which includes the teaching of Jesus Christ and his early followers.

⌃ Jesus is shown in the centre of this stained glass window from a Christian church in Germany.

The spread of Christianity

Christianity was founded around 2,000 years ago. In the 11th century CE, the Christian community split into two main branches, or churches: the **Roman Catholic** Church based in Europe and the Eastern **Orthodox** Churches in Asia. These churches share many beliefs but disagree on others. Further splits in the 16th century CE led to the growth of **Protestant** churches, including the **Anglican** Church that developed in England.

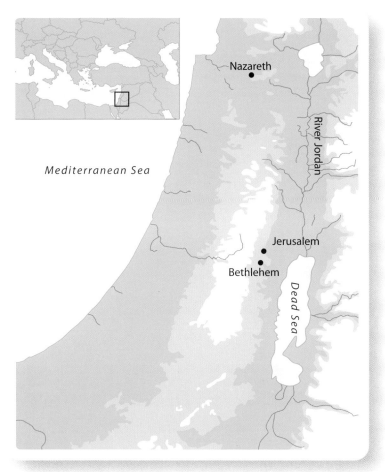

Nazareth

Mediterranean Sea

River Jordan

Jerusalem

Bethlehem

Dead Sea

≫ This is a map of the area in which Christians believe Jesus Christ lived. Today, this area includes Israel and Palestine.

The life of Jesus Christ

Almost all the accounts of Jesus's life come from the four **Gospels** of the New Testament. These were written several years after his death. Christians believe that Jesus's mother was called Mary, but his father was God. Jesus grew up in the area of Galilee, in modern Israel, before **preaching** and performing miracles in the region. He was followed by a group of 12 **disciples**. Jesus's teachings and the way people followed him as a leader angered priests and the Roman authorities who executed him by nailing him to a cross. He was 33. An important Christian belief is that Jesus was able to rise from the dead after three days.

A world religion

There are more than 2 billion Christians around the world. In 2011, more than 33 million people in England and Wales said they were Christian. This is around 6 out of every 10 people. However, only around 1 in 10 people attends a Christian church service every week.

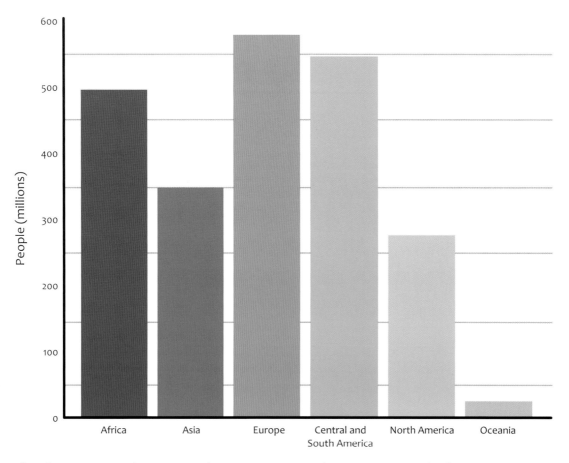

⌃ Christianity is the major religion in Europe, the Americas and Africa.

Festival days

Christians celebrate a calendar of festivals every year. Some of these festivals, such as Christmas, fall on the same date every year. Other festivals, for example Easter, occur on different days.

The most important Christian festivals celebrate events in the life of Jesus Christ. For example, Christmas celebrates his birth, whilst Easter remembers his crucifixion and **resurrection**.

The ways these festivals are celebrated vary between different Christian communities. This is because Christianity has become a part of so many different cultures in different countries around the world.

Holy Communion

During Christian services and at festival times, Christians take part in the **ritual** of **Holy Communion**, also called the Eucharist, Mass or the Liturgy. This dates back to Jesus's Last Supper with his disciples. Christians share bread and wine, which are believed to be or represent the body and blood of Jesus. The Eucharist is central to all Christian churches. Differences in the beliefs about what actually happens in this service have often caused division between branches of Christianity.

CALENDAR OF CHRISTIAN FESTIVALS

This calendar includes the main festivals celebrated by Western Christian churches. The Christian year begins with Advent.

November–December	Advent, beginning with Advent Sunday
25 December	Christmas Day
6 January	Epiphany and the end of 12 days of Christmas
2 February	Candlemas
February–March	Lent, beginning with Ash Wednesday
March or April	Mothering Sunday in the UK on the fourth Sunday in Lent
	Holy Week including Palm Sunday, Maundy Thursday, Good Friday Easter on the first Sunday after the full moon following Spring Equinox, between 22 March and 25 March
May–June	Ascension Day
	Pentecost or Whitsun
1 November	All Saints' Day
2 November	All Souls' Day

Advent and Christmas

If you asked people to name one Christian festival, most would mention Christmas. In Western countries, even people who never go to church celebrate Christmas in some way. For Christians, Christmas marks the birth of Jesus Christ and is a very joyous celebration.

The weeks leading up to Christmas are called Advent. This period is normally seen as the start of the Christian year.

In the Roman Catholic and many Protestant churches, Advent includes four Sundays, and it always ends on Christmas Eve, 24 December. For Orthodox Christians in the East, Advent starts in mid November. The first Sunday of the season is called Advent Sunday. In the past, Advent was a time for not eating some types of food (fasting). This is still the case in Eastern Orthodox churches.

⌃ Traditionally, Christians light candles on an Advent **wreath** to mark the four Sundays of Advent.

Advent calendars

The first Advent calendars were used in the 1800s. Scenes from Bible stories behind each door helped children to learn about the importance and symbols of Advent and Christmas. Nowadays, many Advent calendars have chocolate behind each door, while the pictures behind the doors may have little to do with preparing for the Christian festival of Christmas.

The Second Coming

Advent has another meaning for Christians. The word "Advent" is taken from Latin and means "coming". Some believers use this time to anticipate the Second Coming of Jesus. They believe that when Jesus comes again, this will mean the end of the world. At this time, all people will have to account for the way they have lived their lives.

Celebrating Jesus's birth

For Western Christians, the festival of Christmas lasts for 12 days, from Christmas Eve (24 December) until the evening before 6 January. That day is the festival of Epiphany, when three wise men or kings brought gifts to the baby Jesus. This is why Eastern Orthodox Christians don't celebrate Christmas until 7 January.

The Nativity

The story of the Nativity, or birth, of Jesus Christ first appeared in the Gospels of Luke and Matthew. Jesus was born in a cave or stable in the town of Bethlehem. Luke describes how poor shepherds visited the baby, while Matthew mentions the visit of three wise men. Matthew's Gospel also tells of the family's escape into Egypt. This was after King Herod planned to kill the newborn baby he thought might be a future King of the Jews.

⌃ A crib or scene from the Nativity story is placed in many churches at Christmas.

Some people believe that the Church of the Nativity in Bethlehem stands on the spot where Jesus Christ was born.

Changing meaning of Christmas

Christmas is a time when Christian churches are full. This is particularly true for the traditional service marking the start of Christmas at midnight on Christmas Eve. Christians sing joyful hymns called carols, celebrating the birth of Jesus. They believe Jesus came to save humankind.

Christmas is one of the two most important Christian festivals. However, many Christians believe that the true meaning of this festival has been lost. This is because, for many families, Christmas has become a time to spend lots of money on presents and food. Christians believe it should be about celebrating the life and teachings of Jesus.

⌃ Many families come together to celebrate Christmas.

Christmas traditions

In cold countries like the UK, churches and other buildings are decorated with holly, fir trees and other evergreen plants, which still have their leaves in winter. This tradition also goes back to the ancient festivals that existed before Christmas.

Many of the traditions associated with the festival in the UK were first introduced in the 1800s. This includes Christmas trees, exchanging Christmas presents and sending cards.

Before it became a Christmas tradition, presents were often given at New Year or Epiphany. This still happens in some countries, such as Spain. The tradition may have its origins in the gifts that the three wise men brought for Jesus, according to the Bible.

Food and feasting

Feasting was already part of mid-winter celebrations before Christians began to celebrate the festival. Traditional food is served around the world, but the Christmas meal itself varies. Roast turkey is popular in the UK, but other traditional meals include fish in Sicily, Italy.

⌃ These dancers are performing a Christmas show in Burundi.

There are millions of Christians in Africa. Christmas there is very different from many colder countries. Christmas foods include goat meat in East Africa or fufu and okra soup in Ghana. There is a great emphasis on attending church and celebrating with music. In Malawi, groups of children perform songs and dances. Decorations include candles and bells, but they adorn mango or palm trees rather than fir trees.

Now & Then

Festival of winter

The Bible does not give any date for Christ's birth. Some people think the date of 25 December was chosen by Pope Julius I in the 4th century CE. The date was chosen because it was a time of year when many pre-Christian festivals were already being celebrated. It is just after the shortest day of the year in the **Northern Hemisphere** on 21 December.

Mince
pies

Mince pies are a traditional British treat at Christmas time, dating back to the 1500s. They are filled with apples and sweet dried fruits inside tasty little packages for one! **See page 44 for more cookery tips.**

TIME:

About 1½ hours

SERVES:

12 people (1 pie per person)

TOOLS:

knife and chopping board
zester
weighing scales
saucepan
stirring spoon
rolling pin
13 cm pastry cutter
8 cm pastry cutter
cupcake tray
pastry brush
oven gloves

INGREDIENTS:

3 large apples, peeled and diced
70 g raisins
70 g dried cranberries
70 g dried cherries
zest of 1 lemon
zest of 1 orange
25 g butter
175 g packed dark brown sugar
125 ml apple juice
1 teaspoon cinnamon
¼ teaspoon allspice
¼ teaspoon cloves
¼ teaspoon nutmeg
1 packet of frozen shortcrust pastry
1 tablespoon milk
1 tablespoon granulated sugar

Vegetarian

STEPS:

1 In the saucepan, mix together all the ingredients (except the pastry, milk and granulated sugar). Heat on medium high until the liquid starts to bubble. Then turn down to medium low and let simmer uncovered for about 30 minutes. Let cool.

2 Preheat oven to 230°C/Gas mark 8. Unroll the pastry dough until about 1 cm thick. Cut out 12 large circles and 12 small circles with the pastry cutters.

3 Press the larger circles onto the bottoms and up the sides of the cupcake tray indents. Fill each one with a large spoonful of the cooked apple mixture. Leave a little space at the top.

4 Place the smaller circle on top of the filling.

6 Bake for about 15 to 20 minutes until the crust is golden brown. Let the pies cool completely before removing from the tray.

5 Brush the tops of the pies lightly with milk, and sprinkle with sugar. Cut four small slits in the tops.

LENT

Lent is the period leading up to Easter. The Bible states that Jesus spent 40 days and 40 nights living and praying in the wilderness before he started preaching. During this time, his faith was tested by the Devil. Becasue of this, Lent is a time of reflection for Christians.

Now & Then

Fat Tuesday

The day before Lent is called Shrove Tuesday. In the past, this was the last day that Christians were allowed to eat eggs, milk or butter before the Lent **fast**. These ingredients were used up to make pancakes and this tradition continues today. In French, the day is called Mardi Gras or Fat Tuesday. The days just before Lent are also a time for carnivals, and the word carnival itself has its roots in giving up meat.

⌃ Dancers prepare for the annual carnival in Rio de Janeiro, Brazil, which happens just before Lent. The word carnival comes from "carnevale", meaning "put away meat" in Italian.

In the days of the early Church, Lent was a time for **converts** to prepare to be **baptized** as Christians. This included a period of fasting during the day or avoiding certain foods.

In the past, Christians often stopped eating animal products, such as meat, during Lent. The eating of fish was sometimes allowed, and there was usually no fast on Sundays. Today, Christians are most likely to give up something they enjoy, such as chocolate, as a way of observing Lent. Other people may give money or time to those in need.

Ash Wednesday

For many Christians, Lent starts on Ash Wednesday, about six and a half weeks before Easter. In some churches, the foreheads of worshippers are marked with ashes on Ash Wednesday. Traditionally, these ashes are the burned remains of palm crosses from the previous Palm Sunday (see page 20). The marking of the forehead is therefore a sign of being sorry for **sins** before the start of Lent. In Eastern Orthodox churches, Lent starts slightly earlier but finishes before Easter.

▽ The ashes used on Ash Wednesday remind Christians that they will die one day and their bodies will return to dust.

MOTHERING SUNDAY

Many people do not realize that Mothering Sunday is a Christian festival. In the UK, this is a time for remembering and thanking our mothers with cards, flowers and cakes. In churches, children are given small bunches of flowers to give to their mothers.

Mothering Sunday, or Mother's Day, is now celebrated more widely and not just by Christians.

Uncertain origins

The name of the festival probably comes from an ancient Christian tradition. On this day, Christians from individual **parishes** would go in a procession to what was called their mother church, usually the nearest cathedral. The day had other names in the past. These included Refreshment Sunday because it was a day to break the Lent fast.

In England, celebration of Mothering Sunday goes back at least to the 1600s. On that day, apprentices, farm workers and servants who lived away from home would be given the day off. They could all return home to their families and celebrate with a family meal.

Apprentices would bake a cake using ingredients such as butter that were not usually eaten in Lent. This **custom** gradually died out as jobs like apprentices and servants became less common in English society.

Now & Then

A day for mothers

Mother's Day as we celebrate it today was introduced in the United States in 1914, following a campaign by Anna Jarvis (see picture, right) of Philadelphia. In many countries, Mother's Day falls on the second Sunday in May, so it has no links to the traditional Christian calendar. Briton Constance Smith was inspired by Jarvis. She published a booklet called *The Revival of Mothering Sunday* in 1920. Within a few years, mothers were honoured across Britain.

HOLY WEEK AND EASTER

The final week of Lent in the Western Christian church is called Holy Week. The days of Holy Week follow the events of the last week of Christ's life. The week leads up to the most important Christian celebration of Easter.

Palm Sunday

Holy Week begins with Palm Sunday, which celebrates Jesus's arrival in Jerusalem. According to John's Gospel, crowds waved palm leaves and cheered as Jesus entered the city riding on a donkey. Today, palm or other leaves are waved and churchgoers are often given small crosses, made from palms, at church services.

According to the Bible, many of those who cheered Christ on Palm Sunday were the same people who called for his execution in the same week. Palm Sunday teaching therefore reflects on the challenges of these events.

≫ Palm Sunday is remembered with processions to Christian churches around the world.

Maundy Thursday

The Thursday of Holy Week marks the end of Lent. It remembers the day when Christ ate the Last Supper with his disciples. The Last Supper was the inspiration for Holy Communion. The name "Maundy" comes from an old word for command. This is because it was the day Jesus commanded his followers to love one another.

Maundy Money

In England and Scotland, the king or queen traditionally washed the feet of his or her subjects on Maundy Thursday. This custom ended around 1688. In modern times, the king or queen distributes bags of special coins, called Maundy Money, to senior citizens in a special ceremony.

During the Last Supper, Christ washed his disciples' feet. This was a job normally done by a slave or servant and showed Jesus's desire to serve them. In some churches, a priest or minister will remember this event by washing the feet of 12 members of the **congregation**.

Good Friday

On the night of Maundy Thursday, Jesus was betrayed by Judas, one of his disciples. This betrayal led to Jesus's arrest and trial. The priests saw Jesus as a critic of their power and way of life. The Romans who ruled the region were told Jesus was a rebel.

Jesus was put on trial by the Roman governor. A huge crowd called for him to be executed by being nailed to a cross, a usual Roman way of execution. The cross has since become a central symbol of Christianity.

Good Friday is a solemn day in the Christian calendar, when believers remember Christ's suffering. Traditionally, Christians did not eat meat on this day. Many people still eat fish instead of meat on Good Friday.

▽ Hot cross buns are traditional spiced buns baked for Good Friday in the UK.

Why is it called Good Friday?

Some experts believe that "Good" simply means holy, or that the day was originally called God's Friday. The official explanation in the Anglican Book of Common Prayer states that the day is good because "through his death, [Jesus] opened to us the gates of everlasting life". That meaning becomes clearer with the story of Easter.

≫ Actors perform a passion play in Poland.

Now & Then

Passion plays

The dramatic story of Christ's crucifixion has been an inspiration for art and music for hundreds of years. Local communities in different countries re-enacted the events around Good Friday. Many of these passion plays are still staged today. In the Philippines, one village recreates the crucifixion of Christ with devoted Christians volunteering to be nailed to crosses, although the Roman Catholic Church does not support this as volunteers could hurt themselves.

Easter

Easter is celebrated on the Sunday after Good Friday, but the date varies each year. Easter Sunday can be between 22 March and 25 April. Its date affects when some other festivals are celebrated, such as Lent.

According to the Bible three of Jesus's followers – Mary Magdalene, Mary and Salome – visited his tomb on the third day after his death. The cave where his body had been placed was empty. Jesus appeared to Mary Magdalene and other disciples in the days following this miraculous discovery.

Easter is celebrated with joyful church services and family meals. Each country has its own special Easter dishes. Cakes and breads are particularly popular, such as the Italian Colomba di Pasqua, or Easter dove cake.

♥ Some places, such as this town in Spain, are home to colourful Easter processions, with floats telling the Easter story.

Why is Easter so important?

Easter is the most important festival for Christians because it celebrates Jesus rising from the dead. For Christians, this confirms their belief that Jesus was the Son of God because he could conquer death. It is also the basis for the Christian belief that a person's spirit lives on after death.

Now & Then

Easter eggs

For many people, chocolate Easter eggs are the best-known symbol of Easter. Eggs have been associated with the festival since at least the 13th century CE. Today, we think of Easter eggs as made of chocolate. In the past, they were coloured or decorated real eggs, although some people still paint eggs at Easter today. Traditionally, eggs were not eaten on weekdays during Lent and Holy Week, so eating them at Easter added to the celebration. The egg is also a pre-Christian symbol of new life. It is used by Christians as a symbol of Christ rising from his tomb at Easter.

Green
soup

In Germany, many Christians eat a soup made of fresh greens and herbs on Gründonnerstag – the Thursday before Easter – also known as Green Thursday or Maundy Thursday (see page 21). The greens represent the new life that arrives in the springtime.

For the mixed greens in this recipe, you could use pre-packaged salads from the supermarket. These can include rocket, spinach and watercress. You might also like to use some green herbs, such as parsley.

For more cookery tips for this recipe, turn to page 44!

TIME:

15 minutes

SERVES:

4 people

V Vegetarian

G Gluten Free

TOOLS:

kitchen scales
teaspoons
measuring jug (to measure the broth)
knife and chopping board
food processor
large saucepan
stirring/wooden spoon

INGREDIENTS:

3 large handfuls (about 200 g) of mixed greens with herbs (see note, above)
1 litre chicken or vegetable broth (you could use a stock cube)
20 g unsalted butter
3 spring onions, white and greens, sliced
½ teaspoon salt
½ teaspoon pepper
sour cream and chopped fresh parsley for garnish

STEPS:

1 In a food processor, blend together the salad greens with about a quarter of the broth until smooth. Set aside.

2 In the large saucepan, melt the butter on medium-high heat. Add the spring onions and sauté for about 2 minutes until slightly browned.

3 Add in the rest of the broth, the puréed greens, and the salt and pepper. Bring to a boil, then reduce the heat. Cover and let simmer for about 5 minutes.

4 When serving, garnish with a spoonful of sour cream and a sprinkling of fresh parsley.

Ascension Day and Pentecost

On Good Friday and at Easter, Christians celebrate the death and resurrection of Jesus Christ. However, this is not the end of the story. Ascension Day and Pentecost are two festivals that celebrate what Christians believe happened next.

Returning to heaven

The Bible records how Jesus appeared to his disciples after rising from his tomb. Forty days later, according to Mark's Gospel, Jesus returned to heaven and to God. This is marked by Ascension Day, which is 40 days after Easter Sunday. The day is sometimes called Holy Thursday (not to be confused with Maundy Thursday).

《 In the past, Christians thought that God's heaven was just beyond the sky they could see.

Ascension Day is celebrated by all branches of Christianity. In the Eastern Orthodox churches, it is one of the most important festivals of the year. In countries where most people are Roman Catholic, Ascension Day is a public holiday.

Some traditional ways of marking Ascension Day are no longer followed today. One of these is the ceremony of raising a cross or statue up through a hole in the church roof, which was popular in medieval times.

Now & Then

Beating the bounds

At one time, the days before Ascension Day in the UK were marked by processions around the local area or parish. These processions led to the tradition of beating the bounds. A group of people from each town or village would walk around the boundaries of the parish to mark where they were. Children would go, too, so that knowledge of the parish boundaries was passed on to the next generation to settle any future arguments with neighbouring parishes. This tradition still happens today in some places, such as Oxford (picture below).

Pentecost

Ten days after Ascension Day is Pentecost Sunday. Pentecost is the birthday of the Christian church. Christians believe that Christ's disciples were visited by the Holy Spirit and started to tell others about the teachings of Jesus Christ. We know that this festival has been celebrated in some form since the 2nd century CE at least.

According to the Bible, the disciples were celebrating a Jewish festival together when they heard a sound like a rushing wind. The disciples saw tongues of fire and began to speak in foreign languages, which would help them spread the word of Christ. Christians call this power the Holy Spirit and it is seen as God's power.

White Sunday

In the UK, White Sunday – also known as Whitsun – is another name for Pentecost. The festival falls in May or June. It was a time for great feasts and fairs in the past, as well as a popular time for baptisms. No one can be quite sure where this name came from, but it could refer to the white robes worn by babies ready for baptism.

Pentecostal churches

There are many different Protestant churches. Some of these are often called Pentecostal churches, particularly in the United States. Pentecostal churches believe that all their members can have a religious experience similar to the one felt by the first Christians at Pentecost, called baptism with the Holy Spirit. They believe that Christians who have been baptized in the Holy Spirit can start to speak in languages that they did not know before. They may also gain special healing powers.

Pentecost is a happy time. Here Pope Francis, head of the Roman Catholic Church, is wearing red robes to represent the fire of the Holy Spirit.

HARVEST FESTIVAL

There have been festivals to celebrate a successful harvest since people first began to grow crops. These types of festivals are part of every religion. For Christians, harvest festivals are some of the most popular celebrations. Churches are decorated with fruit, wheat and other crops.

There is no set date for harvest festivals in the Christian calendar. This is partly because the dates of harvest vary in different countries. Christians mark the harvest with special church services or assemblies in schools. In the UK, these are usually held in September.

The tradition of these services in churches only goes back just over 150 years. Worshippers bring food to the church and schools. They also collect food, which is later donated to people in need or to senior citizens. In the past, this food was usually fresh, but nowadays many people bring in tinned foods.

⌃ This church has been decorated for a harvest festival.

Thanksgiving

The festival of Thanksgiving is celebrated across North America in October and November. Today, this holiday is a time for most Americans and Canadians to spend time with their families, eating roast turkey and pumpkin pie. The festival began as a Christian harvest festival when Protestant settlers celebrated their first successful harvest in 1621.

⌃ An American family celebrating Thanksgiving.

Now & Then

Lammas

In centuries past, when most people worked on the land, the harvest was a major event of the year. Lammas was the annual "loaf festival", celebrated in August in England. A loaf made from the first corn to ripen would be blessed in church.

ALL SAINTS AND ALL SOULS

In the New Testament of the Bible, all the early Christians are called **saints**. Later the word is used to mean special holy people. Many saints died for their beliefs.

Protestants tend not to separate these people out for special attention. However, Roman Catholic and Orthodox Christians observe many special saints' days.

On 1 November, Roman Catholics and Anglicans celebrate the lives of saints and people who have died for their Christian beliefs. This is called All Saints' Day. Methodist Churches celebrate the lives of all members of the church on All Saints' Day, as they consider all members of the church to be saints. Eastern Orthodox churches celebrate the saints on the Sunday after Pentecost.

≫ St Paul was one of the most important people in the early Christian Church. He spread the word of Jesus and wrote several books of the Bible.

Praying for souls

All Saints' Day is followed by All Souls' Day, on 2 November. This is a time for people to pray for the souls of "the faithful departed", or Christians, including family members, who have died. It is a holiday in many Catholic countries. Mexicans celebrate two Days of the Dead at this time of year and exchange gifts. They visit family graves with picnics and leave food for the souls of their dead loved ones.

⌃ On the Days of the Dead, Mexican mourners light candles on the graves of their loved ones.

Now & Then

All Hallows' Eve

All Saints' Day used to be called Hallowmas, and the night before was called All Hallows' Eve or Halloween. Halloween is when the souls of the dead were supposed to be active and visit the living. This festival is still a celebration of all that is ghostly and gruesome, loved by children in many parts of the world. It has lost most of its links to Christianity.

Pan de
muerto

Pan de muerto is a food made for Day of the Dead in Mexico. Its name means "bread of the dead". Families place this bread on altars for their loved ones.

See page 44 for more tips, including how to knead bread!

TIME:
About 3½ to 4 hours

SERVES
8 people

TOOLS:
weighing scales
small saucepan
stirring/wooden spoon
mixing bowls
clean tea towel
oven tray
baking paper
oven gloves
pastry brush
cooling rack

INGREDIENTS:
60 g unsalted butter
80 ml milk
80 ml water
400 g plain flour (plus more for dusting)
7 g (1 packet) yeast
¼ teaspoon salt
60 g caster sugar
1 tablespoon fennel seeds
2 large eggs, slightly beaten
Glaze: 40 ml orange juice, 30 g caster sugar

 **V** Vegetarian

STEPS:

1 Heat the butter, milk and water in the saucepan on medium-low for about 5 minutes until the butter melts. Set aside.

2

In a large bowl, combine 150 g of the flour with the yeast, salt, sugar and fennel seeds. Pour in the liquid mixture. Add the eggs and mix well.

3 Add another 150 g of flour and stir to combine. It should form a dough. Add the rest of the flour a little at a time, stirring well after each addition.

4 Dust a work surface with flour. Then scrape the dough out onto it and knead for 10 minutes.

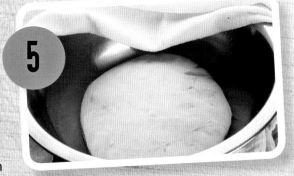

5

Place the dough into a bowl greased with butter. Cover with the tea towel. Put it in a warm place for about 1½ hours until it has doubled in size.

6 Punch down the risen dough, and turn it onto a floured work surface. Pinch off a small handful. Divide the rest into four round loaves and place them on an oven tray lined with baking paper.

7 Shape the reserved dough into eight bones. Cross two bones on the top of each loaf.

8 Cover the loaves with the tea towel, and let them rise, for about 1 hour. Bake at 180°C/gas Mark 4 for about 15 minutes until golden brown.

9 Make a glaze by mixing the orange juice and sugar in a small saucepan. Heat on medium for about 5 minutes until the sugar is dissolved. Brush onto the warm loaves. Cool the bread on a cooling rack.

FAMILY CELEBRATIONS

Christians go through different stages in their relationship with the church. These ceremonies or **rites of passage** are often marked with joyful family celebrations.

Baptism

To become members of the Christian community, people go through the ceremony of baptism. In most cases, Christian families arrange for their young children to be baptized. The child is baptized with water and blessed by the priest. The child's parents and godparents - a couple chosen from the parents' friends and relatives - make a promise to bring the build up in the Christian faith. Godparents promise to bring the child up in the Christian faith. The newly baptized baby is given cards and presents by family and friends.

Baptism of Jesus

The Bible tells us that Jesus was himself baptized in the River Jordan by John the Baptist. Some Protestant churches therefore believe that converts should be baptized similarly, by being fully submerged in water. According to Matthew's Gospel, Christ urged his followers to baptize members of the church.

Some Christian churches believe that new members should be old enough to make their own promises to the church. Baptist churches therefore baptize their members when they become adults.

Confirmation

Members of the Anglican and Roman Catholic Churches are usually baptized as children. The next stage is the ritual of confirmation.

Confirmation takes place at any age. However, it usually happens when people are old enough to understand what it means to be a Christian. They need to make their own commitment to live a life according to Christian values. Candidates usually take classes to learn what this means. In the Anglican Church, confirmed members are then able to take part in Holy Communion.

⌃ The Church of England states that anyone in preparation for confirmation can receive communion as part of that preparation.

Christian weddings

Marriage is one of the most exciting and momentous events that many people go through. Different Christian groups have slightly different wedding ceremonies. But, generally, Christian couples choose to celebrate their marriage in a church or another special holy place, so they can make their **vows** before God.

For example, Anglican marriages normally take place in the local church of either the bride (woman) or bridegroom (man). Before the wedding, their marriage will be announced during church services in their home parishes on three separate Sundays. This gives others an opportunity to object to the marriage if they think there is a problem, for example if one member of the couple is already married to someone else!

Wedding traditions and their meanings

Christian wedding ceremonies are full of symbols that reflect the values of marriage. For example, after making their vows the couple exchange rings to show their commitment to each other. The priest or minister blesses the marriage, and the couple and witnesses sign the parish register. A party usually follows this ceremony.

♡ The exchanging of rings is one of the most important moments the ceremony.

Wedding traditions and customs vary between churches and countries: in the Orthodox churches, couples wear crowns. Some branches of Christianity, such as Quakers, have more relaxed wedding ceremonies, with fewer symbols and rituals. The couple sometimes exchange rings but this is not required.

▽ This couple are wearing crowns at an Eastern Orthodox wedding ceremony.

Divorce

For Christians, marriage is a **sacred** bond that is meant to last a lifetime. Churches discourage divorce. However, the Church of England was founded because of a divorce. King Henry VIII (who ruled between 1509 and 1547) wanted to divorce his first wife and marry someone else. The Roman Catholic Pope was not happy with this. However, Henry divorced Catherine, anyway. Eventually, the King made himself head of a new Church of England in 1534.

A WORLD OF CHRISTIAN FESTIVALS

Festivals such as Christmas and Easter are shared by Christians around the world. But many Christians also celebrate local festivals.

Timkat

For hundreds of years, the Christian Church of Ethiopia was separated from most other Christians because Ethiopia was surrounded by lands that followed Islam. The Church therefore developed many of its own traditions and celebrations. Timkat, the Ethiopian version of Epiphany, is the biggest festival of the year. It begins with noisy and colourful processions, followed by a baptism ceremony that recalls Jesus's baptism by John the Baptist.

⌃ Colourful and joyous processions are important features of the Timkat festival in Ethiopia.

Saints' days

Festivals for individual saints are part of the Eastern Orthodox and Roman Catholic calendars. Saints are less important to Protestant churches, which believe that Christian faith should be about following the teachings from the Bible and not worshipping saints. However, many countries and communities will often mark the days of their own patron saints.

The patron saints of the UK and Ireland are:

- St David (patron saint of Wales, celebrated on 1 March): he was an important figure in the early Christian church in Wales.
- St Patrick (Ireland, 17 March): he helped to convert Irish people to Christianity.
- St George (England, 23 April): a soldier probably born in Turkey, who supposedly killed a dragon. However, he never came near England, as far as we know.
- St Andrew (Scotland, 30 November): he was Jesus's first disciple, whose bones were believed to lie in Scotland.

These patron saints are remembered with processions, special services and distinctive crosses on flags.

⌃ England's flag is the cross of St George (on the left), and Scots (above) wave the cross of St Andrew.

Cookery tips

Green soup

- Sautéing cooks vegetables over high heat with a little bit of fat, such as vegetable oil. It browns the vegetables and brings out their flavours before you add other ingredients.

Mince pies

- To zest orange or lemon peel, clean the outside of the fruit with water. Use a grater with small holes to take off small bits of the fragrant outer peel. Don't grate too deep – the white part is bitter.

- Dried spices can lose their smell and flavour if kept too long. The best place to store them is a kitchen cupboard. Spices stay freshest in dry, cool places out of sunlight.

- When rolling pastry dough, spread flour on your work surface and rolling pin first. This will prevent the dough from sticking. But try not to add too much flour. It can dry out your dough.

Pan de muerto

- To knead dough, place it on a floured work surface. Fold the dough in half, and then flatten and stretch it with the heel of your hand (see picture, right). Repeat until the dough is smooth and stretchy.

TIMELINE

BCE

c. 4 BCE	Likely date for birth of Jesus Christ, not 1 CE as originally calculated in the Christian calendar

CE

c. 30 CE	Jesus Christ dies and is resurrected, according to Christian beliefs
47–c.64	St Paul is active in setting up the first Christian churches
65–95	Four Gospels recounting the life of Jesus are written
Before 100 CE	Roman invaders and traders bring the story of Jesus to Britain for the first time
221	First mention of 25 December as the date of Jesus's birth
312	Constantine I becomes Roman Emperor, later ending persecution of Christians and converting to Christianity himself
325	First Council of Nicea agrees many of the core beliefs of Christianity, including deciding when Easter should be celebrated
597	St Augustine of Canterbury establishes the Roman Catholic Church in Britain
1054	The Eastern Orthodox and Roman Catholic churches split in what is called the Great Schism
1517	Criticism of the Catholic Church, led by German monk Martin Luther, causes the founding of Protestant churches, in what became known as the Reformation
1534	King Henry VIII breaks from the Catholic Church and becomes leader of the Church of England
2013	Pope Francis becomes the first leader of the Catholic Church from South America

GLOSSARY

Anglican member of the Church of England or any related church, or describing anything to do with these churches

baptism special ceremony in which a new member is accepted into a Christian community

congregation collective name for the people who attend church

convert someone who has changed to a particular religion

custom act or way of living that is traditional

disciple follower. People who followed Jesus during his lifetime were called disciples or apostles.

fast go without food or drink for a particular period of time

Gospel one of four accounts of the life of Jesus that are included in the Bible

Holy Communion (also called the Eucharist) ceremony or ritual that is a central part of Christian worship, in which Christians are given bread and wine to remember Jesus's Last Supper with his disciples

Northern Hemisphere area of the Earth found north of the Equator

Orthodox name for churches that are descended from the Eastern churches that separated from the Western church in the 11th century CE

parish area, such as a town or village, with its own church building and clergy

Pope leader of the Roman Catholic Church

preach talk to people about religion

Protestant member of one of the Christian churches that broke away from the Roman Catholic Church during the 1500s, or of churches that have been set up since that time

resurrection coming back to life after being dead

rite of passage ceremony marking someone's change from one stage of life to the next, such as a wedding

ritual religious ceremony or custom

Roman Catholic person or church that is a member of the largest Christian community, following Roman Catholic teachings and recognizing the authority of the Pope

sacred something which is connected with God or otherwise seen as holy

saint person who is recognized by a church for having lived a particularly good or holy life

sin bad deed, or one that breaks the rules set down by a religion

spiritual deeply held belief, which can be religious

vow solemn promise

wreath flowers or leaves fixed together on a ring and used as a symbol at festivals or to remember a dead person

Find out more

Books
Christianity (Special Times), Catherine House (A & C Black, 2013)
I am Christian (Talking About My Faith), Cath Senker (Franklin Watts, 2010)
A Year of Christian Festivals, Flora York (Franklin Watts, 2013)

Websites
www.bbc.co.uk/schools/religion/christianity/index.shtml
The BBC schools website has a section covering Christianity and its festivals.

www.whyeaster.com/customs/passionplays.shtml
This website gives information about Easter and related special days, covering everything from passion plays to Easter eggs.

www.factmonster.com/ipka/A0882306.html
The Fact Monster website includes details of special days for many different religions, including Christianity.

Places to visit
If you live in a country with a large Christian community, you can probably find out more about the religion and its festivals by visiting your local church. Churches are often decorated at festival time, and many churches are open to visitors most of the time. You should always be quiet and respectful in any place of worship.

Further reseach
- This book has only been able to cover some of the differences between how different Christian churches celebrate festivals. Look more closely at the festivals of the Roman Catholic or Eastern Orthodox churches, or at the traditions of churches in Africa or the Middle East.
- Christian beliefs and the life of Jesus have inspired centuries of paintings, sculpture and music in Europe and elsewhere. Discover more about Christian art in churches and museums.
- Investigate Christmas and Easter traditions in your country and community. How do people in your local area celebrate these festivals? Which traditions are directly related to Christianity, and which have other sources?

INDEX